Smart cards.

TELEPHONE CARDS

Yves Arden

Additional material by Andrew Emmerson

Photographs by Sophie Lee

Shire Publications Ltd

CONTENTS

Published in 1994 by Shire Publications Ltd, Cromwell House, Church Street, Princes Risborough, Buckinghamshire HP27 9AA, UK.
Copyright © 1994 by Yves Arden. First edition 1994. Shire Album 304. ISBN 0 7478 0253 X.

Printed in Great Britain by CIT Printing Services, Press Buildings, Merlins Bridge, Haverfordwest, Dyfed SA61 1XF.

British Library Cataloguing in Publication Data: Arden, Yves R. Telephone Cards. – (Shire Albums; No. 304). I. Title. II. Series. 769.5. ISBN 0-7478-0253-X.

ACKNOWLEDGEMENTS
Thanks are due to Andrew Emmerson for his help with the text; to Sophie Lee for the trouble she took in providing the photographs and many cards used in this book; to David Beresford and Laura Lee for the time they spent in collecting cards from so many different places; and to Alan Collenette of Guernsey Telecoms, Eleanor Hardy of Cambridge Telephones, Peter Damsberg of Kite Communications Ltd and Terry Twible of T & T Sales for the help and information which they have so generously provided.

Mercury's distinctive payphones are now a common sight in British towns and cities. From the outset they were designed to accept only cards, not cash.

The BT Museum special phonecard in its original sachet; unopened cards are more valuable.

PAYPHONES — CASH AND CARDS

Collecting phonecards is a fascinating and instructive hobby; it costs very little to start but can become extremely expensive if one gets addicted! It is one of the fastest growing pastimes, yet for most British collectors it started only in 1981, when British Telecom introduced the first cashless cardphone. Like postage stamps, telephone cards are colourful and plentiful and are used in many countries of the world. They cost little to collect, yet increase in value and, as designs and patterns change, cards that were once easily obtained soon become collector's items.

What is the fascination? The reason is simple. More than three hundred telephone companies and administrations in 165 countries now issue phonecards and many of these cards, especially the early issues and short-run 'specials' produced to promote products or commemorate events, are short-lived. They are easy to obtain at the time but then become well-nigh impossible to find and start appreciating in value rapidly.

Remarkably, most people just throw used cards away, which means that one can start a collection at minimum cost. Many rarities have been found discarded outside payphones simply because some people do not use up their cards immediately. This is almost the only way that very early issues still turn up. Particularly

prized by collectors are the special issues used in prisons and on offshore oil rigs, and the 'personal' cards printed as business cards to be given away by senior telephone-company executives.

In Japan the hobby is almost as popular as stamp collecting, with new issues coming out regularly. Phonecards are becoming equally popular in Britain and the United States of America and the hobby is growing fast in the Middle East, Latin America and Africa. Phonecard collecting falls neatly between coin and stamp collecting and might well overtake them in popularity.

The aim of this book is to help beginners in this fascinating hobby to start their collections, to give them some general advice and ideas on how to acquire cards and how to store and display them. It is impossible here to catalogue all the cards issued — there are too many already — but some of the many catalogues that are available are listed at the end of the book.

The terms 'fusilately' and 'telegery' may sometimes be encountered. These are the official or 'serious' names given to the hobby of collecting phonecards, although some collectors consider these names ridiculous and see no need for bogus respectability. This book uses the simpler and more obvious term 'phonecard collecting'.

HISTORY OF PAYPHONES

Public telephones are over a hundred years old. The first one in Britain was installed in Bristol in 1886. Originally the user paid for the service in a shop or elsewhere or gained entry to a booth by a penny-in-the-slot lock. Soon special coinbox telephones were devised. In other countries, such as France and Italy, tokens or *jetons* were sold for use in payphones, reducing their susceptibility to theft. Paying for calls in advance by buying a telephone card was first introduced in Belgium in the 1970s and in Britain in 1981. The price per unit varies worldwide, but in the United Kingdom a BT unit costs about 10p in 1994.

British Telecom (BT) has over 100,000 public payphones, of which nearly 25,000 accept phonecards. (Some also accept bank credit cards and telephone-company charge cards.) Mercury Communications Ltd continues to install payphones using both phonecards and charge cards. A more recent development has been the managed payphone system, which is a public telephone on private premises such as hospitals, universities and schools.

In the 1970s the Landis & Gyr company developed card-operated telephones in co-operation with the Belgian telephone administration. At that time there were no high-value coins in Belgium, so that it was very inconvenient to make long-distance or foreign calls from payphones. As these cards proved more convenient than coins or tokens and reduced the incentive to vandalise telephone boxes the idea soon proved popular and most countries use them now.

Collecting phonecards as a hobby started in Japan. The exchange of gifts is very frequent in Japan and the Nippon Telephone and Telegraph company (NTT) had the brilliant idea of promoting its cards as gifts. People quickly started to collect them. Special cards could be produced to order in quantities as low as a hundred, which resulted in a huge variety of cards, and most of these are never used since the Japanese collect only cards in mint condition. There are countless attractive designs and so many of them — forty thousand different designs of card have been mentioned — that the Japanese catalogue listing them comprises several volumes.

In many countries telephone cards started in the early 1980s with a utilitarian design in a single colour (for cost and technical reasons). BT chose green; red was used in Belgium and Switzerland, orange in Austria, purple in Spain, blue in France, Portugal and Sweden. Soon these were followed by a wide range of multicoloured illustrated cards, some commemorative, others for advertising or promotional purposes and some for private use. Some of these are aimed more at the collector than the user. Telephone cards are produced in vast quantities: in the United Kingdom BT issues twenty million cards annually, to which those of other operators must be added.

ALL KINDS OF CARDS

There are two other kinds of 'phonecard' besides the prepaid cards for using in payphones. One is the telephone credit card ('charge card' or 'calling card') issued by BT, Mercury and many other telephone administrations. These cards are normally supplied free with no subscription cost: the user is subsequently billed according to the use he or she has made of the card. The cards are magnetic, often of attractive design, and they tend to look very similar to normal phonecards, the only difference being that calls are paid for after rather than before they are made. Many of these cards work in several countries. WorldPhone, for instance, issued by the American operator MCI, is claimed to be the world's first global telecommunications brand that provides international callers with savings.

The second kind is the smart card used in the new GSM pan-European digital mobile telephones. Only one smart card is issued to each subscriber, so this type is not easy to come by; they look very similar to the smart cards used with the more advanced payphones and bear the name of the mobile-phone operator. Telephone tokens, which look rather like coins, are covered later in the book.

BT first series definitive: this was the only one to use the word 'cardphone'.

BRITISH TELEPHONE CARDS

British Telecom started to issue phonecards in 1981. These were green and silver and are known to collectors as 'basic green cards' (BGCs) or 'definitive cards'. In 1987 BT produced its first special cards. These were followed by the first commemorative card, which was a multicoloured card for Christmas 1987.

BT DEFINITIVE CARDS

The term 'definitive' is taken from stamp collecting and means the standard issue. So definitive cards are the commonest types of card, which have undergone various design changes over the years. Some complimentary cards of 3, 5 and 10 units were given away by BT for promotional purposes, and some of these cards have been used by firms as an incentive to respond to their advertising. Altogether there have been nine different designs of basic green cards.

The first series (1981-5) is easily distinguishable by the caption on the front, 'For conditions see cardphone leaflet', as this was the only time the word 'cardphone' was used. The second series (1984-5) has the name 'Phonecard', which was to remain, and a slightly different design. Cards in the third series (1987) used the same design but with a notch on the right of the card to help blind people to insert the card correctly. What is generally known as the fourth series (1988-9) included cards made in Switzerland and in Britain; the Swiss cards are now hard to find.

The fifth series (1990) was printed by the offset process except the silk-screened optical strip. The wording on the card was in white instead of silver, with a green background, and the silver border remained. The sixth series (1990) was on sale only for a trial period, offering free units with the cards. The seventh series (1991) can be distinguished by the legend at the bottom left-hand corner in which the new BT emblem replaced the words 'British TELECOM'. In the eighth series (1992) the optical strip is white instead of green, with instructions printed on the reverse for the first time. The ninth series

5

BT second series definitive. Note the subtle changes in design.

BT third series definitive.

BT fifth series definitive.

BT sixth series definitive. By now BT was using more imaginative designs.

BT seventh series definitive with the new piper emblem.

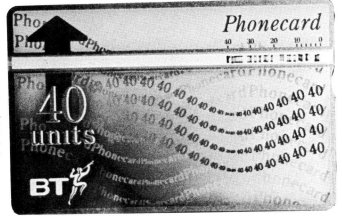

BT eighth series definitive. A numbered strip helped users check the value remaining. Note how used units show as black marks.

(1993) is similar, but the cards have a new silver border.

In 1994 a tenth series was launched which is green and red and repeats the idea of the sixth series of giving bonus units. New definitive cards are sold in a sealed plastic envelope called a sachet, to assure purchasers the card is unused. New cards are more valuable to collectors if they are still in the sealed sachet.

SPECIAL AND COMMEMORATIVE CARDS

These were first issued in 1987 for the Open Golf Championship at Muirfield and then for the British Telecom London Challenge for Students. They were green and silver, of special design, and only a small quantity was issued; they are now rare and expensive. At Christmas 1987 and on St Valentine's Day 1988 BT first issued

Four BT complimentary cards.

8

BT Christmas 1988 20 and 40 units cards with special envelopes. These were intended to be used as gifts.

BT 20 units card for the Wimbledon tennis championships, 1990. A similar card was issued in 1991 with the new logo.

Left: *Two cards from BT's 1989 winter set of five.*

Right: *BT winter 1990 cards from a set of five; complete sets are more valuable than individual cards.*

BT World Student Games, 1991, in original sachet.

commemorative cards through its normal outlets; these were multicoloured and generally very attractive. Other designs followed.

ADVERTISING CARDS

The number of these cards has been growing very quickly. They include give-away gimmicks, rewards for responding to advertisements and promotions requiring customers to collect labels or tokens.

Originally promotional cards were available only to people responding to the promotion, but some (not all) can be bought through the BT Collectors Club.

Well-known manufacturers issued these advertising cards: Nescafé, 40 units (1991), and Kellogg's Cornflakes, 20 units (1992).

11

PRIVATE CARDS

These are promotional cards which are not offered to the public but are produced for firms using them as visiting cards to give to customers or to include in information folders. Several senior executives in British Telecom have their own visiting cards printed on phonecards, for instance. Other cards are sold above face value as fund-raisers for charities and by enterprising dealers who produce cards with attractive pictures purely for sale to collectors.

PRISON SERVICE CARDS

These are BT cards used in prisons in the United Kingdom. At first they were ordinary BT cards with a handstamp to show that they were for prison use. They

are rather expensive and a number of forgeries exist. They were replaced in 1989 by special 20 units cards in green and blue with the wording HM PRISON SERVICE. The design was changed in 1992 and the wording altered to FOR USE IN HM PRISONS ONLY. Cards for the Scottish Prison Service, of different design, but also green and blue and of 20 units value, were introduced in 1991. Prison cardphones do not accept normal phonecards and these special cards are sold only to prisoners, making them very hard to find in unused condition.

OFFSHORE PLATFORM CARDS

These cards are used on offshore oil and gas platforms by the employees of the various exploitation companies such

BT private card. The eleventh Christmas Pudding Race, 20 units.

BT private card for Selfridges in its original sachet.

These BT cards are the only ones which can be used in prisons. They are impossible to obtain unused (except by prisoners).

For information on any Mercury Communications service call 0800 424194

as British Gas, Britoil, Shell, BP and North Sea Sun Oil Company. Originally utilitarian cards in red or green, these now sport various designs, including some multicoloured pictures. Some are quite expensive to obtain.

ENGINEERS' TEST CARDS

Special cards are issued to BT payphone engineers for testing payphones. These are hard to obtain but are sometimes found discarded at cardphones.

MERCURYCARDS

Mercury Communications Ltd, Britain's other national telephone company, launched its payphones in 1988, initially in London. Its payphones can now be found in many town centres, stations and airports. Very few take cash but they all accept credit cards and the company's own Mercurycards.

Mercurycards differ from BT phonecards in many ways. They are magnetic, not optical, which means that there is no visual difference between used and unused cards. Mercurycards have been multicoloured from the start and almost all of them are pictorial; they form a very attractive collection with great scope for thematic collecting (wildlife, trains, aeroplanes, ships, buildings, et cetera).

The majority of Mercurycards can be considered 'specials' and there is also a vast number of private cards, either advertising cards or limited issues produced for special events, and even visiting cards for named individuals promoting their company or services. Yet other cards are produced specifically for collectors and are very unlikely to be used. In 1994 there were over four hundred of these.

THE MAIN CORPORATE CARDS

The first issue (1988) comprised pictorial cards showing Mercury payphones and with the caption 'First — 1988 issue'. This was followed by a Waterloo station card, multicoloured and very attractive; the 1988 Christmas issue of London views; and in 1989 five cards for the introduction of Mercury payphones in Birmingham, Bristol, Edinburgh, Glasgow and Manchester. For Christmas 1989 a set of five cards was issued showing various pantomimes, followed in 1990 by a map of the London Underground, of which there are two slightly different patterns. The Prince's Trust set of three cards showing Phil Collins and Harry Enfield (who plays the Mr Grayson character in Mercury's television commercials) came in 1991, and then a set of three cards, again with Harry Enfield, showing how easy it

Left: *Two cards from the Mercury set of six 'More colourful ways to call'* .
Right: *Mercurycards for Christmas 1988.*

Many Mercurycards carry attractive designs in colour.

This set of five pantomime cards from Mercury was issued in a folder.

Harry Enfield played 'Mr Grayson' in Mercury's advertising campaigns. These cards are known as the Simple, Push and Insert set.

Two Mercurycards advertising hotels.

Mercury sent its subscribers this card as a VAT refund.

is to use Mercurycards and known as the Simple, Push and Insert cards. There are two types, one with a plain back and the other printed on the reverse.

It is impossible to give details of all the private cards, but themes included ships, trains, aviation, hotels, wildlife and stores. An interesting collection is the cards issued under a scheme sponsored by leading companies in February 1991 to pay for £10 Mercury cards for free issue to the forces engaged in the Gulf War, enabling them to make free home calls. A contribution of £10,000 would buy one thousand cards, each paying for two or three short calls or one eight-minute call home. The scheme was run on a non-profit basis through payphones operated by Cable & Wireless, Mercury's parent company, in Saudi Arabia and the Gulf area. British Aerospace, National Westminster Bank and Cable & Wireless together contributed £1 million to purchase 100,000 cards. Other firms followed, and the total quantities issued were fairly large, but it is hard to tell how many were lost or wasted after use. So far they are still relatively inexpensive.

Mercury persuaded major corporations to sponsor free telephone calls for British forces engaged in the Gulf War.

17

Paytelco: two cards from the Boots series.

PAYTELCO CARDS

These cards are issued in a joint operation between Mercury and Paytelco (a subsidiary of GPT Ltd, who make Mercury's payphones). They are issued through multi-site organisations and they are particularly well-known for the Shell series. The other main series are: Boots, showing different services of that company; Trust House Forte, advertising their Travelodge and THF services; the Post Office, whose first set was three sportsmen (Colin Jackson, Andy Ashurst and Dalton Grant), followed by a Beryl Cook set of four. The Post Office also issued, in conjunction with the Capital Gold radio station in London, a set of five photographs of disc jockeys given away as competition prizes. Paytelco has also issued four thematic sets: wildlife, pop stars, Olympic Games themes and the Territorial Army.

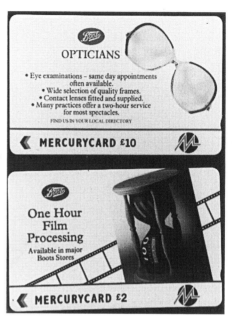

Paytelco: two cards from the Post Office's first set of sportsmen and one from the second Beryl Cook set.

FOOTBALL AND UNIVERSITIES

Football cards were issued originally in £2 and £5 denominations for the majority of the Football League and Scottish clubs. Some club cards were also issued in packs of two which sold at a small premium over the £7 face value. As many cards were left unsold, these were later devalued and overprinted £2. These make a large and interesting thematic collection.

Following the same pattern, a series of university cards, starting in 1991, has been issued and continues to be added to. Paytelco also has some private cards issued to customers in limited quantities, either for advertising or for the collectors' market.

OTHER BRITISH CARDS

Another telephone service is the managed payphone facility installed in universities, schools, hospitals, leisure and shopping centres. These public telephones on privately owned premises usually accept cash as well as the company's own telephone cards. These are issued in small numbers compared to the cards of BT and Mercury and their relative scarcity makes them an interesting field for collectors.

International Payphones (IPL) issued complimentary and definitive cards in 1989. They are pictorial and multicoloured. The company ceased to trade in 1991 and manufacture of its equipment was taken over by Integrated Information Technologies (IITL), which in turn ceased trading in 1992. All the manufacturing rights were purchased by Cambridge Telephones Ltd (CTL).

At first some cards were overprinted for the YMCA in Glasgow and for Loughborough University Students Union. Later cards were printed for Loughborough, Reeds School, Ashworth Hospital and other customers. There is a collectors' service.

International Payphones Scotland (IPLS), originally part of IPL, started to produce its own cards in 1991. These included some for offshore platforms, Edinburgh Tattoo, Dundee University and others.

Kite Communications Ltd issues its own cards with different illustrations of a red kite on a silver and blue background, as well as a test card, of which only a small quantity was produced. There is a service for collectors.

CHANNEL ISLANDS AND ISLE OF MAN

Guernsey Telecoms introduced new technology in its payphone system in 1993 by having 125 public telephones accepting cash, credit cards and their own smart telephone cards. To launch the new system, a set of cards in a presentation pack was issued and made available through seventy retail outlets with the incentive of extra free calls. The cards illustrate in colour the various types of public telephones used in Guernsey. A second set of cards, with multicoloured pictures of Castle Cornet, was launched in May 1994. There is a collectors' club.

Jersey has issued cards since 1988. Very attractive multicoloured cards have been issued in sets since 1990, each with a different theme: castles, locomotives, wildlife and so on. There have now been twenty different issues, which offer great opportunities for the thematic collector. A few advertising cards have also been issued.

Manx Telecom issued green and silver definitive cards in 1987 but soon changed them to multicoloured pictorial cards, which form a very attractive collection. There is also a growing number of commemorative and special cards, usually issued in sets: several were for the TT races, while others illustrated such themes as local stamps and transport. There are good facilities for collectors.

One of the many pictorial cards issued in Jersey.

Used Christmas 1992 cards from Australia showing the perforations made in used cards.

FOREIGN TELEPHONE CARDS

Over one hundred different countries issue telephone cards, and in some of them, as in the United Kingdom, there are several companies producing cards. Whilst generally there is a range of basic definitive cards, there is often a proliferation of multicoloured pictorial cards commemorating various events, illustrating scenery or wildlife, or promoting some particular cause, as well as advertising, personal, test and service cards and so on.

To help identify foreign cards, there is a glossary at the end of the book. It is not possible to give details here of all countries issuing cards, but here are a few notes on the countries whose cards are most likely to be come across.

AUSTRALIA

Since the first trials in 1989-90, Telecom Australia has issued sev-

Humorous cards from Australia advertising the service.

20

Thematic collecting. Good examples of wildlife cards from Australia.

eral series of attractive pictorial cards, and its collectors' club is very informative. Cards are punched as they are used, so it is easy to distinguish unused ones.

AUSTRIA

Telephone cards have been available since 1981. When calls are made a white band on the cards is marked in black. There have been several definitive issues with modified designs in orange or green. There are also a number of advertising cards, mostly multicoloured, and a few service and test cards.

BELGIUM

Belgium made an early start with telephone cards in 1977-9 and these are now valuable. There have been a number of definitive issues, which are red and of varying designs. Marks on a red strip show when the card has been used. Since 1988 there have been various issues of commemorative, special and advertising cards which are multicoloured.

CYPRUS

The Cyprus Telecommunications Authority (CYTA) has issued a range of attractive multicoloured pictorial cards which have been widely used by tourists and which are readily available.

DENMARK

There are four companies issuing cards; the first was KTAS, the Copenhagen telephone company, followed by Jydsk in Jutland and later Fyns Telefon and TS. Most of the cards are pictorial and multicoloured.

FINLAND

Only a few of the many telephone companies in Finland have issued cards, which are definitive single-colour blue cards and pictorial multicoloured ones.

FRANCE

France Télécom started to issue telephone cards as late as 1980, but it has become the second largest issuer of cards, after Japan, and there is a very large number of collectors. Different systems have been used and there is a vast number of definitive optical, magnetic and electronic cards manufactured by different companies and using different systems. Definitive cards fall loosely into two types: those illustrated with stripes and called 'pyjamas' in France; and those showing a telephone instrument and a length of cable, called 'cordons'. These have been followed by a multiplicity of pictorial cards, some commemorative, some thematic and others advertising. A wide range of subjects is illustrated and it is a fascinating collection, but somewhat daunting because of its size.

GERMANY

After a period of trials in selected areas in 1983-4, using different systems, a range of definitive cards was started in 1986. These are red on white and gold on white. They were followed by a wide range of multicoloured advertising and private cards, covering many subjects.

GREECE

Greece started to issue pictorial multicoloured cards in 1987.

HOLLAND

Definitive cards started in 1986 and there have been several series with design modifications. These were green, and without a notch, until 1988. Several issues have cards of higher value with a bonus added. Advertising is usually on the back of the cards.

HONG KONG

Trial cards were first issued in 1984 and since 1990 there have been many special cards, all multicoloured pictorials covering a wide range of subjects and

Four cards from the vast range issued in France.

22

Holland: two cards from a thematic set on football.

A complimentary card used to advertise the service in Hong Kong.

very attractive. There are good facilities for overseas collectors.

IRELAND

After extensive trials in Dublin, Galway and Limerick in 1989-90, Telecom Eireann now issues a wide range of attractive cards and has excellent facilities for overseas collectors.

ITALY

Cards have been issued since the late 1970s. A special feature is that one corner has to be removed before use. In the first system cards used were retained by the apparatus, which makes the earlier cards difficult to acquire. Until 1986 cards were printed vertically, but they have since become horizontal. There are a number of definitive issues of varying designs and colours. Since 1990 there have been a large number of tourist authority issues depicting various areas of scenic interest.

These are usually in sets of three cards including a free card. Collectors may be confused by the fact that some cards have a German text for use in the German-speaking area of the South Tyrol (Alto Adige); generally these have been issued in smaller numbers. Some rare cards, without value, were issued for use in the parliament building.

JAPAN

Telephone-card collecting began in Japan and it is the largest issuer of telephone cards. Because of the huge range (forty thousand different cards and a catalogue in several volumes, in Japanese) it is not possible to give here even a general view of these cards but NTT has issued cards for Japanese nationals travelling abroad and these have been on sale in Geneva, London and New York. They are 50 units, pictorial and multicoloured.

Because the Japanese are interested in

Three telephone cards from Italy showing how the corner is cut off when the cards are used.

collecting only unused cards, many of their used cards are readily available in other countries.

MALTA

Definitive cards of 50 units (red) and 100 units (blue) of classical design have been issued by Telemalta Corporation.

MONACO

Definitive red cards of 50 and 120 units were introduced in 1987 and there have been several series of these, varying in the type of contact. Since 1989 multicoloured commemorative and private cards have been issued.

NEW ZEALAND

After trials in 1989, definitive cards were issued, multicoloured pictorials showing a satellite dish. Since then there have been a number of sets of very attractive multicoloured cards.

PORTUGAL

CTT has issued definitive cards of standard blue and silver design with a white strip indicating when they have been used. Telefones de Lisboa e Porto SA have also issued cards which are of very similar designs. Commemorative and advertising cards have now been issued by both organisations.

SPAIN

Following trials in 1981, definitive cards of classical design were issued in 1986. Multicoloured pictorial cards followed in 1989 and then commemorative ones.

SWEDEN

Whilst a universal system has not yet been adopted, there are cards for special use in hospitals and military installations. One special type is the cards sold on trains for use in train telephones.

24

Malta: definitive 100 units card.

Definitive New Zealand $2 card showing satellite dish (second issue).

Portugal uses this definitive 120 units card.

25

SWITZERLAND

Definitive cards were first issued in 1982; they are red, of classic design. There are also a number of private multicoloured pictorial and advertising cards not sold to the general public. There are some rare cards used for official purposes and for closed user groups.

Some foreign cards also carry slogans: these are examples from France, Austria and Australia.

BUILDING A COLLECTION

WHAT TO COLLECT

Whilst it is tempting for the beginner to collect all cards, it will soon become obvious that a more selective approach is needed. There are a number of options. You may decide to collect only United Kingdom cards, or even to specialise only in BT phonecards, Mercurycards or others. If you want to collect foreign cards as well, here are a few categories: cards only from countries you have visited; cards from countries where you have friends or business connections prepared to send used cards; cards from countries which cater for overseas collectors, where the telephone service has a collectors' club, a new issue service and a newsletter (some countries are very good at this, and a list is given at the end of the book; as only unused cards are sold and there is a handling charge, they can be expensive); cards from a country such as Guernsey, which was late in starting to issue cards, and where a complete collection can be achieved quite cheaply; cards which form a thematic collection ignoring frontiers, which offers great possibilities, depending on your interests.

HOW TO OBTAIN CARDS

New cards can of course be bought. BT has a collectors' club and it is understood that the collectors' service Mercury had until 1992 will be available again shortly.

Unused cards which are no longer current can be purchased from dealers, from auctions or obtained from other collectors through a club exchange service. Used cards can be found in many public telephones; not all users are collectors. They can also be obtained from friends and acquaintances. Several charities like Oxfam sell them to raise funds.

Foreign cards can also be purchased from dealers in Britain.

CONDITION

The golden rule is to collect only cards in good condition unless they are very rare. Often users, when they finish with a card, bend it in half and this is impossible to straighten out without leaving some marks. Cards which are scratched or disfigured should be discarded or ignored.

UNUSED OR USED CARDS?

While Japanese collectors collect only unused cards, in other countries more used cards are collected. When they can be easily distinguished, unused cards are normally more valuable than used ones on account of their better condition. In many cases it is difficult to distinguish between unused and used cards without expensive equipment or trying them in a payphone. Unused BT cards can be distinguished by the absence of marks on the optical strip and by the sachet, if present.

Collecting only unused cards is more expensive as some have a face value of £20. On the other hand, buying them unused is often the only way to get commemorative or special cards. So the beginner's choice will depend very much on his budget and also on his contacts for used cards.

OTHER ITEMS TO COLLECT

Some collectors also include in their collections the envelopes used by BT, the teaching kits (with a complimentary card) issued to schools, the various folders containing special sets of cards, such as Christmas sets, or advertising material. Another area is the printers' proofs in official folders which are issued for approval prior to acceptance, and these generally relate to private cards.

A growing specialism, for the more advanced collector, is dealing with the serial numbers on the backs of the cards. These are sometimes upside down in relation to the text on the front of the card, or they are left out or different codes refer to printings made at different times. Specialised catalogues give much detail in this field, and keen collectors may sift through thousands of cards looking for rare variations. There may also be different messages, some advertising or in-

Always check the back of phonecards: here are advertisements on some BT and Paytelco issues.

structions for the use of the card on the reverse, whilst others are blank. So it is always worth looking at both sides of a card.

STORING A COLLECTION

Dealers sell special loose-leaf albums with clear plastic sheets of pockets to hold cards. The pockets are too small to accommodate the BT sachets, however, and cards may fall out. Small photograph albums with clear plastic pockets can be used successfully, especially for cards in envelopes. The best way to display cards is in a picture frame with an easily removable back, covered with baize.

PUBLICATIONS

Catalogues and magazines are listed at the end of this book. The various collectors' clubs issue illustrated lists of new cards at regular intervals and these are very useful for keeping up to date. Most card dealers issue price lists which contain a great deal of useful information and also indicate the current values of cards on the market.

TELEPHONE TOKENS

Telephone tokens, the predecessors of phonecards, are metallic objects of bronze or cupro-nickel, looking rather like coins. They were used in Britain during the early days of public telephones and remained in use for many years in other countries. In France they are called *jetons* and there were variants, usually with similar-sound-

ing names (for example the Italian *jettone telefonico*) in other European countries. The French ones carried a bust similar to that on coins, and nearly all tokens had a groove or keyway cut in them, which helps identification. These tokens are generally considered of trifling value by coin collectors, so it may be possible to obtain them cheaply from coin dealers.

28

GLOSSARY

Some cards show no country of origin and this list of names may help identify them.

Argentina: *tarjeta telefonica*
Australia: *phonecard*
Austria: *Telefonwertkarte*
Belgium: *telecard*
Brazil: *cartao telefonico*
Cyprus: *telecard*
Denmark: *telekort*
Finland: *pukelukortti*
France: *télécarte*
Germany: *Telefonkarte*
Guernsey: *phonecard*
Holland: *telefoonkaart*
Ireland: *callcard*
Italy: *carta telefonica*

Korea: *teleca*
Luxembourg: *telekaart*
Malaysia: *kadfon*
Malta: *telecard*
Norway: *telefonkort*
Portugal: *credifone*
Sweden: *telefonkart*
Switzerland: *taxcard*
Turkey: *telefon karti*
United Kingdom: *phonecard*
United States of America (New York): *change card*
Yugoslavia (former): *telekarta*

Ships are always a good subject for thematic collecting.

FURTHER READING

Emmerson, A. *Old Telephones*. Shire Publications, 1978; reprinted 1990. History of telephones and payphones in general.

Hiscocks, S.E.R. *The Collector's Book of Telephone Cards*. World Telephone Card Publications, 1989. A full-colour guide showing all the main designs from Britain and other countries around the world, together with their values.

Hiscocks, S.E.R. *The Stanley Gibbons Catalogue of Telephone Cards*. Stanley Gibbons, second edition, 1990.

Hiscocks, S.E.R. *Collect British and Irish Telephone Cards*. Stanley Gibbons, 1991.

Hiscocks, S.E.R. *Telephone Cards of the World. Part I: Great Britain and Ireland*. World Telephone Card Publications, fourth edition, 1993.

Johannessen, Neil. *Telephone Boxes*. Shire, 1994. The history of telephone kiosks in Britain up to the present.

Britain's Public Payphones — A Social History. BT, 1984, reprinted 1990. Detailed history of the payphone.

Fabulous Phonecards: An Introduction to Phonecard Collecting. BT, 1995. Free colour booklet issued by BT.

Your Guide to Phonecard Collecting. Telecom Australia, 1991.

Most of these publications are available at The Story of Telecommunications (BT Museum), 135 Queen Victoria Street, London EC4V 4AT. There are also several specialised catalogues dealing with individual countries and usually published abroad.

The following periodicals are very useful:

International Telephone Cards: bi-monthly, from the publishers, ITC, 29/35 Manor Road, Colchester, Essex CO3 3LX. This magazine also has details of collectors' fairs.

Telecard Collector International: monthly from newsagents or from Castle House, 97 High Street, Colchester, Essex CO1 1TH.

The private card of Landis & Gyr, who developed card-operated telephones in the 1970s.

CLUBS FOR COLLECTORS AND TELEPHONE-CARD SALES OFFICES

Some official collectors' clubs and telephone authorities' sales offices for collectors (information subject to change).

AUSTRALIA
International Telephone Card Society (ITCS), Telecom Australia, PO Box 3964, Parramatta, NSW 2124, Australia.

BAHRAIN
Bahrain Telecommunications Company, Operations Service Controller (DQ2), PO Box 14, Manama, State of Bahrain.

FIJI
Fiji Post and Telecom (Phonecard Collecting), PO Box 40, Suva, Fiji.

FRANCE
Bureau National de Vente des Télécartes, BP 456, 54001 Nancy Cedex, France.

GERMANY
Zentraler Kartenservice Telekom, Deutsche Bundespost Telekom, Fernmeldeamt 2 Nürnberg, Postfach 44 33 22, 8500 Nürnberg, Germany.

GIBRALTAR
International Sales Manager, *Gibraltar NYNEX Communications Ltd*, Suite 942, Europort, Gibraltar.

GUERNSEY
Guernsey Phonecard Club, PO Box 297, Guernsey, GY1 5RX.

HONG KONG
Phonecard Collectors Club, Hong Kong Telecom, PO Box 9896, GPO, Hong Kong.

IRELAND
Telecom Eireann, CallCard Collectors Club, 3rd Floor, 5 Dame Lane, Dublin 2, Ireland.

ISLE OF MAN
Manx Telecom Phonecards, Queen Victoria House, 41/43 Victoria Street, Douglas, Isle of Man.

MALAYSIA
Telekom Malaysia Bethad, Payphone Division, 16th Floor, Wisma Telekom, Jalan Pantai Baru, 59200 Kuala Lumpur, Malaysia.

NEW ZEALAND
Telecom PhoneCard Collector Service, PO Box 3838, Auckland, New Zealand.

NORWAY
Telekort Norge Collector Service, PO Box 23, N-5673 Strandvik, Norway (telephone

00 47 5 584921, fax 00 47 5 584920). Supplies phonecards from Denmark, Finland, Iceland, Norway and Sweden, and also catalogues for these. Send IRC for details.

SWEDEN
Telefinans AB, Phonecard Collectors Service, PO Box 7474, S-103 92, Stockholm, Sweden. Sells Swedish phonecards, colour catalogue.

UNITED KINGDOM
BT Phonecard Collectors Club, PP 550, Camelford House, 87 Albert Embankment, London SE1 7TS. Telephone: 0800 838775, 0171-587 8858 or 0171-587 8126. Send large self-addressed envelope for booklet *Fabulous Phonecards*, catalogue and their information exchange leaflet on how to contact other collectors in the United Kingdom and abroad.
Cambridge Telephones Card Collectors Club, Sterling House, Harding Way, St Ives, Cambridgeshire PE17 4WR.
D & G Phonecard Club, 4 Margaret Street, Hollinwood, Oldham, Lancashire OL8 4SN. Also arranges monthly weekend swapmeet in Timperley.
Kite Communications Ltd, 2 The Courtyard, High Street, Brampton, Huntingdon, Cambridgeshire PE18 8ES.
Mercury Phonecard Collectors Club. This is expected to be re-established. Ring Mercury on 0171-528 2000.
Telegraph and Telephone Study Circle, Box 62, York YO1 1YL; also Box 5627, Hamden, Connecticut 06518, USA. The circle exists to bring together all those with an interest in the history of the telegraph and telephone, with particular reference to methods of prepayment (stamps, franks and phonecards) and ephemera (forms, publicity material, et cetera). Members are kept informed through a quarterly journal *Across the Wire*. The circle also acts as a phonecard exchange club for those who require it.
Telephone Card Club, Box 708, London SE25 6BN.

Information on swapmeets, videotapes, British and foreign dealers and other overseas administrations issuing phonecards can be found in *International Telephone Cards* magazine. In addition to the organisations listed above, many dealers offering phonecards will be found at toy and stamp collector swapmeets which are held all over Britain and advertised in local newspapers and *Exchange and Mart*. National fairs include the National Vintage Communications Fair, held in May at the National Exhibition Centre (NEC) near Birmingham and the Giant Toy and Train Collectors' Fairs held regularly at the NEC, Gateshead International Stadium (Tyne and Wear) and Donington Park (Leicestershire).

PLACE TO VISIT

The Story of Telecommunications, BT Museum, 145 Queen Victoria Street, London EC4V 4AT. Free information line: 0800 289689. Other enquiries: 0171-248 7444. Open weekdays but not Saturday and Sunday.